JUJUTSU KAISEN

6

BLACK FLASH

STORY AND ART BY GEGE AKUTAMI

—CURSE—

Hardship, regret, shame... The misery that comes from these negative human emotions can lead to death.

During the Goodwill Event, Itadori faces off against one of the most ferocious Jujutsu fighters of all—Aoi Todo. Meanwhile, the Tokyo School uncovers a plot by the Kyoto School to assassinate Itadori, leading to an all-out brawl between the students. During the chaos and confusion, Mahito and a crew of mysterious special grade curses attack the students!

Jujutsu High
First-Year
Megumi Fushiguro
Jujutsu High
First-Year
Nobara Kugisaki
Special Grade
Jujutsu Sorcerer
Satoru Gojo
Jujutsu High
Third-Year
Aoi Todo

JUJUTSU KAISEN

6

BLACK FLASH

WHY DOES EVERYONE...
...TORMENT MOTHER?
Chapter 44: Kyoto Sister-School Goodwill Event— Team Battle, Part 11
BECAUSE SHE IS A BROKEN MISTRESS.
THEN WHY DO YOU FAVOR ME?
WHY DECEIVE ME INTO BECOMING THE HEIR?!
BECAUSE THE RIGHTFUL WIFE COULD NOT GIVE BIRTH TO A SON WHO POSSESSES A CURSED TECHNIQUE!
THEN AS THE HEIR TO THE HEAD OF THE KAMO FAMILY...

CH-K
Chapter 44:
Kyoto Sister-School
Goodwill Event—
Team Battle, Part 11
FWIP
SWISH
!!
TP
TP

KA
KRAK
CHK
A SHIKIGAMI USER WHO CAN HOLD HIS OWN IN CLOSE COMBAT... HOW VALUABLE!
YOU'VE GROWN. THAT MAKES ME HAPPY.
WHY ARE YOU ACTING ALL FAMILIAR WITH ME?
IT'S SYMPATHY.
YOU WILL ONE DAY BECOME THE PILLAR THAT SUPPORTS THE BIG THREE FAMILIES.

I...
...INTEND TO KILL YUJI ITADORI!
BY PRINCIPAL GAKUGANJI'S ORDER?
NO. THIS IS MY DECISION.
AS A MEMBER OF THE KAMO AND THE BIG THREE FAMILIES...
...I BELIEVE IT IS THE RIGHT DECISION.
YOU...
I MUST PLAY THE PART OF THE HEIR TO THE KAMO FAMILY.
...SHOULD ALSO UNDERSTAND.

YOU AND I...
FOR MOTHER'S SAKE!
... ARE THE SAME!
NO, WE'RE NOT.
HE'S SAYING SOME SCARY STUFF...
YES, WE ARE.
NO, WE'RE NOT!
PLEASE... YOU SHOULD BRING THAT KIND OF STUFF UP WITH MAKI.
I NO LONGER HAVE ANY CONNECTION WITH THE ZEN'IN FAMILY.
BESIDES, I'VE NEVER THOUGHT OF MYSELF AS DOING THE RIGHT THING.

ACTUALLY, I'M SORRY.
I DON'T CARE IF I'M RIGHT OR WRONG.
I ONLY BELIEVE...
...IN MY CONSCIENCE!
I WILL FOLLOW MY CONSCIENCE AND SAVE PEOPLE.
IF YOU DISAGREE WITH THAT THEN...
LET'S AGREE...
...TO CURSE EACH OTHER!
DO
OM..

FSH
A SHIKIGAMI! IT WAS STILL AROUND?!
PSHH

HE USED A WOUNDED SHIKIGAMI AS A DECOY?!
THIS USES A LOT OF CURSED ENERGY ...
...SO I CAN ONLY SUMMON IT ONCE.
KSSHH
IT ONLY RECENTLY SURRENDERED TO ME.
VNN
VNN
PUFF
MAX ELEPHANT

IT'S A LARGE TARGET!
I HAVE TO INITIATE THE ATTACK!!
SPLASH
!!
WATER?!

KRASH
I'M BEING SWEPT AWAY BY THE VOLUME AND PRESSURE!
NO, I'M WIDE OPEN NOW! IT'S COMING!
VVNNNN

NUE!
GLARE
AA
FWW
AAK
ACK!
KRK

IF I'M AROUND...
...I'LL ONLY GET IN YOUR WAY.
I...!
BLOOD MANIPULATION
FWISH
SPLASH

KRAK
CRIMSON BINDING
THUD
THK
I CAN'T AFFORD TO LOSE!!

WHA–?!
RRRMBBBB
WHAT IS THAT?!
!!
INUMAKI SENPAI?!

RUN...
KRASH
...A...
...WAY!

GLOOM
OH?
GETTING EXCITING, HUH?
BUT CURSED SPIRITS...
...DON'T LEAVE ANYTHING BEHIND WHEN THEY DIE.
I CAN'T MAKE ANYTHING FROM THEM...
HUP!
...CAN I?!
KRAK

AND THEN... UM...
OH, RIGHT. THAT.
EMERGE FROM DARKNESS, BLACKER THAN DARKNESS.
PURIFY THAT WHICH IS IMPURE.
GLOOP
AH, GOOD GOOD.
THE HANGER RACK... HOW EXCITING!

SUPPLEMENTARY INFO ①

On this page, Kamo mentions something about how Nue can't be used in narrow spaces, but... ➡

...in chapter 1, Fushiguro tries to use it in a school's narrow hallways. ⬇

⬅ He was attempting to summon Nue to free himself from the curse's grip.

KAMO THINKS THAT NUE SHOULDN'T BE USED IN CRAMPED SPACES BECAUSE IT'S A LARGE TARGET THAT CAN EASILY BE TAKEN OUT BEFORE IT HAS A CHANCE TO PICK UP SPEED. IN FACT, DEPENDING ON HOW IT'S USED, NUE CAN BE EFFECTIVE EVEN IN NARROW CONFINES.

CHAPTER 45: SAGE

SHZZZ...
GAME OVER...?
AND ALL TOKYO RED?
STRANGE.
MY CROWS HAVEN'T SEEN ANYTHING EITHER.
I'D LIKE TO SAY, AS THE GTG—GREAT TEACHER GOJO—THAT MY STUDENTS EXORCISED THEM.
BUT EVEN WHEN EXORCISED WITH NON-REGISTERED CURSED ENERGY, IT'LL BURN RED.
IT MUST BE AN OUTSIDER. MAYBE AN INTRUDER?
DOES THAT MEAN MASTER TENGEN'S PROTECTIVE BARRIER ISN'T WORKING?

INTRUDER OR NOT...
...THIS IS AN UNEXPECTED SITUATION.
THEY'RE SKILLED ENOUGH TO BE ABLE TO EXORCISE IT.
WHO COULD IT BE?
I'M HEADING OVER TO MASTER TENGEN.
SATORU, YOU GO WITH PRINCIPAL GAKUGANJI TO RESCUE THE STUDENTS.
MEI WILL STAY HERE AND TRY TO GET A LOCK ON WHERE THE STUDENTS ARE LOCATED.
PLEASE LET SATORU AND THE OTHERS KNOW AS SOON AS YOU FIND OUT.
UNDER-STOOD.
I'LL BE EXPECTING A BONUS.
LET'S GO, GRANDPA! TIME FOR YOUR WALK!
CLAP
CLAP
YOU HAD YOUR LUNCH ALREADY, REMEMBER?
IGNORE!
LET'S HURRY.

EMERGE FROM DARKNESS, BLACKER THAN DARKNESS.
PURIFY THAT WHICH IS IMPURE.
BRMBBB

RRRMMBBBB

IS THAT A CURTAIN?!
WHY NOW?!
GOJO! BEFORE THE CURTAIN FULLY FORMS...
...YOU GO ON AHEAD!
NO CAN DO.
WHAT?!
ACTUALLY, THE CURTAIN IS ALREADY COMPLETE. IT'S PRIORITIZING THE CURSED TECHNIQUE'S EFFECT OVER ITS VISUAL.
OUT
IN
Ground
TYPICAL CURTAIN
OUT
IN
Ground
THIS CURTAIN
NOT BAD...
WELL...
KSHH

VWOOOOO
WE'LL JUST RIP IT APART AFTER IT'S COMPLETED.
FSH
SPARK

...?
WHAT IS THIS WEIRD FEELING?
HEY.
GLOOP
WHY DID YOU GET REPELLED ...
...AND I DIDN'T?
UTAHIME AND GRAMPS, YOU TWO GO AHEAD.
THIS CURTAIN...
I SEE.

IN EXCHANGE FOR DENYING SATORU GOJO ENTRANCE...
...IT GIVES EVERYONE ELSE FREE ACCESS!
!!
IN THAT CASE, THE BALANCE BETWEEN GIVE AND TAKE MAKES SENSE.
BUT A CURTAIN THAT CAN SINGLE OUT A SPECIFIC INDIVIDUAL WOULD TAKE A VERY SKILLED...
THERE'S A VERY SKILLED CURSE USER OUT THERE.
AND THEY SEEM TO HAVE A FAIR AMOUNT OF INFO ON US.

C'MON, GET GOING ALREADY. I DUNNO WHAT THEIR OBJECTIVE IS...
...BUT IF EVEN A SINGLE PERSON DIES, WE LOSE.
VOOOO
WHY IS THERE A CURSED SPIRIT HERE?
AND WHOSE CURTAIN IS THAT?
IT'S PROBABLY COMING FROM WHOEVER IS WORKING WITH THIS CURSED SPIRIT.
KOFF!
HUH? YOU KNOW SOME-THING?

THESE ARE UNREGIS-TERED SPECIAL GRADE CURSED SPIRITS!
AND THEY SEEM TO BE WORKING WITH A CURSE USER!
I THINK IT'S THE SPECIAL GRADE CURSED SPIRIT THAT ATTACKED GOJO SENSEI BEFORE.
IT MATCHES THE DESCRIPTION.
I CAN TELL EVEN FROM THAT GUY'S DRAWING.
TUNA MAYO.
YES, YOU'RE RIGHT.
LET'S CALL GOJO SENSEI.
WAIT A MINUTE...
YOU CAN UNDERSTAND WHAT HE'S SAYING?
DOES THAT MATTER RIGHT NOW?
IT MIGHT USE DOMAIN EXPANSION ON US.
WE NEED TO CONTACT GOJO SENSEI AND...

...RETREAT—
FWK
KRAK

DON'T MOVE!
HALT
RR
RIP
BLOOD MANIPULATION
VNN VNN

SLICING EXORCISM!!
THWAK
FWWW
NO DAMAGE?!

DOOM
WHAK
WHAK

THUNK
TCH!
IT'S TOUGH.
WHERE WAS HE HIDING THAT SWORD?

STOP IT, FOOLISH CHILDREN!
WHAT THE—?! I CAN UNDERSTAND...
...THE MEANING BEHIND THE NOISES IT MAKES?
THIS IS CREEPY...
ALL I WANT ...
...IS TO PROTECT THIS PLANET.

IT'S THE CURSE TALKING NONSENSE! IGNORE IT!
IT'S NOT JUST A LOW-LEVEL CURSE THOUGH.
THE FOREST, THE SEA, THE SKY... THEY'RE CRYING FROM THE TRAGEDIES THEY'VE WITHSTOOD.
WE CAN NO LONGER LIVE IN PEACE WITH HUMANS.
THEY KNOW THAT THERE ARE HUMANS WHO CARE FOR THE PLANET.
BUT HOW USEFUL IS MERE COMPASSION?
ALL THEY WANT IS TIME.
THEY'VE FORMULATED THEIR OWN LANGUAGE.
GET INUMAKI OUT OF HERE...
WITH THAT TIME, THE PLANET WILL ONCE AGAIN SHINE A BRILLIANT BLUE.

TIME...
RMMMBBLL
...WITHOUT HUMANS!
THOU SHALT BECOME A SAGE...
...THROUGH DEATH.

SUPPLEMENTARY INFO ②

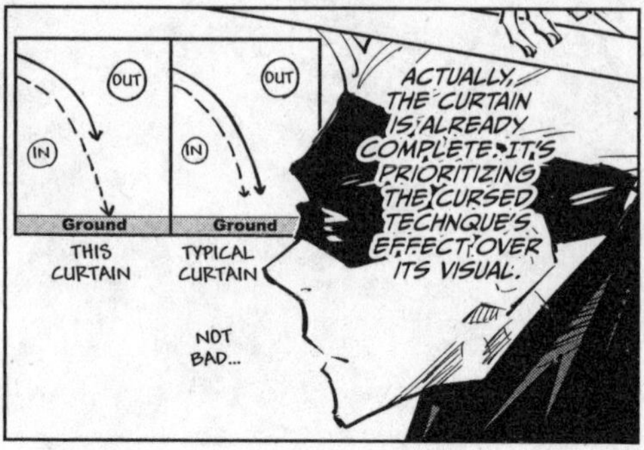

← The "visual" mentioned here is referring to the blinding effect on sorcerers, but what about non-sorcerers?

• Non-sorcerers (those who can't see curses) are able to be killed by curses, thus are able to touch curses. But they generally won't notice if they are touching or are being touched by curses. (That depends on the individual.)

• In the same vein, non-sorcerers cannot see curtains, so they see through them. And no matter what happens inside the curtain, they won't notice.

• So, for non-sorcerers, the blinding visual effect is more like "no awareness."

THE GRAPHIC DRAWN INCLUDES THE GROUND TO MAKE IT EASIER TO UNDERSTAND, BUT A CURTAIN EXTENDS INTO AND IS JUST AS EFFECTIVE UNDER THE GROUND.

Chapter 46: Time

GLOOP...
TCH!
VEEN
I CAN FEEL THE HEAVY PRESENCE OF CURSES! COULD IT POSSIBLY BE A SPECIAL GRADE?
HEY, HEY, HEY!
HEY, HEY, HEY, HEY!!

WHERE IS SATORU GOJO?!
A CURSE USER. YOU'RE NOT THE MAIN PRESENCE I FELT, BUT YOU'RE PRETTY SKILLED TOO.
THAT DEPRAVED MONK...
HE TRICKED ME!
UTAHIME, LEAVE THIS TO ME.
SAVING THE STUDENTS IS OUR PRIORITY. DON'T FIGHT IF YOU DON'T HAVE TO.
WAIT A MINUTE! AT LEAST LET ME KILL THE WOMAN!
KLAK
I CAN'T MAKE ANYTHING OUT OF SOME OLD GEEZER'S HOLLOW BONES AND WRINKLED SKIN!
HOLLOW, HUH?

WHY DON'T YOU KILL ME...
...AND FIND OUT HOW HOLLOW MY BONES REALLY ARE?!
GET BACK TO ME AFTER YOU DRINK SOME MILK!
YOU ROTTING GEEZER!

KRAK
KRAK
KRAK
ARE YOU OKAY, INUMAKI SENPAI?
GLUG
SALMON.
FSH
HERE IT COMES!!

STOP!
THUNK
THUNK
THUNK
HALT
HALT
HALT
HALT

CONVER-
GENCE!
SPLI
SH
PIERCING
BLOOD!
FWI
NG
WH
ACK

KRMBL
!
HE MANAGED TO HURT IT! WAS HE JUST GOING EASY ON ME?
HURRY! IT'LL HEAL AND BE AFTER US AGAIN SOON ENOUGH.
KOFF!
LOZENGE
WE'LL HAVE INUMAKI STOP IT SO WE CAN KEEP SOME DISTANCE BETWEEN US AFTER WE ATTACK!
WE GOTTA DO THIS IF WE'RE GONNA HAVE A CHANCE OF GETTING OUT OF THE CURTAIN. WE NEED TO FIND THE PRINCIPALS.

BUT HOW LONG CAN WE KEEP THIS UP?
INUMAKI'S CURSED SPEECH IS LOSING EFFECT. WE CAN'T GET IN TOUCH WITH THE TEACHERS EITHER.
IT MAY EVEN FIGURE OUT A WAY TO COUNTER CURSED SPEECH.
THE CURSE'S OBJECTIVE REMAINS A MYSTERY.
THERE'S A CHANCE THE PRINCIPALS AND THE OTHER JUJUTSU SORCERERS ARE IMMOBILIZED.
FINDING TODO IS A PRIORITY. EVEN MIWA WOULD DO AT THIS POINT.

VOOM VOOM VOOM VOOM
INUMAKI SENPAI WILL STOP IT.
DON'T BE AFRAID.
RUB
FOO
SH

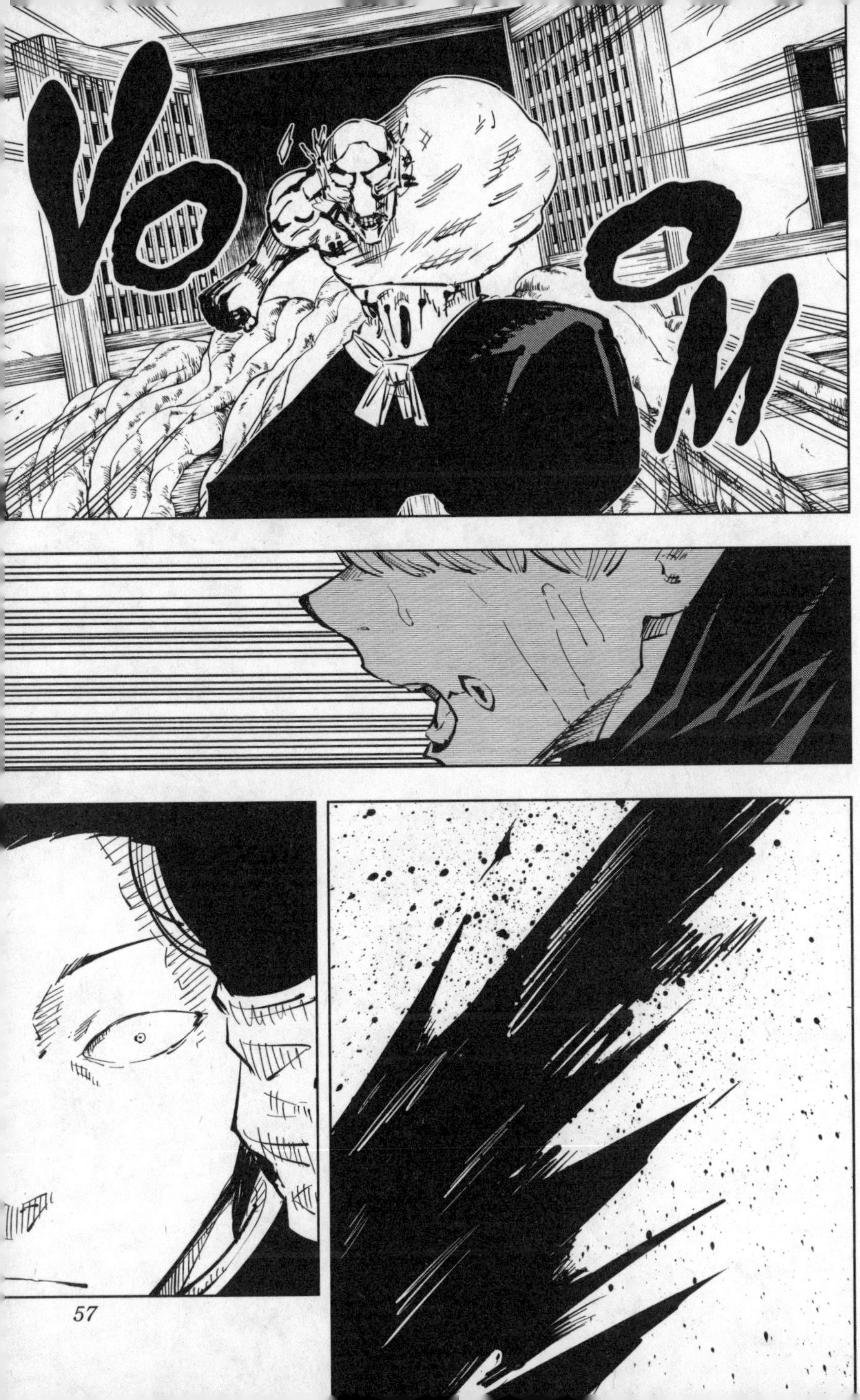
VOOOM

SHNK
PLIP
PLIP
PLIP

INUMAKI REACHED HIS LIMIT FIRST!
WHAM

FWING
FWING
FWING
WHAM
WHAM
KAMO!! YOU STILL ALIVE?!

THE CURSED SPEECH HE USED WASN'T PARTICULARLY STRONG, BUT HIS THROAT GAVE OUT. THE ENEMY IS THAT MUCH...
...STRONGER!
!!
PAT
PICKLED MUSTARD LEAF.

INUMAKI SENPAI!!
ANY MORE AND YOU'LL–
FSH
FSH
FSH
FSH
BLAST...
...AWAY!

KRAMBL
YOU CAN'T CUT ME WITH SUCH A SWORD.

TCH!

ITS EYE BRANCHES ARE ITS WEAK POINT!
GU GU GU...
THAT ONE'S BLADE ISN'T SO WEAK.
I'VE GOT SOMETHING EVEN BETTER.

BUT USING THIS...
KLANK
...JUST DOESN'T FEEL RIGHT!
FW
SH

POP QUIZ JUJUTSU ASSESSMENT

Question 1
(answer required)

Why did Maki Zen'in not feel right in this panel? Choose the most appropriate answer. (10 points)

(A) - Because it's the same tool Geto used in volume 0 to beat her up.

(B) - Because if you look closely, it looks like three fluorescent tubes, which is uncool.

(C) - Because she just remembered Mai never called her "big sis" and that annoys her.

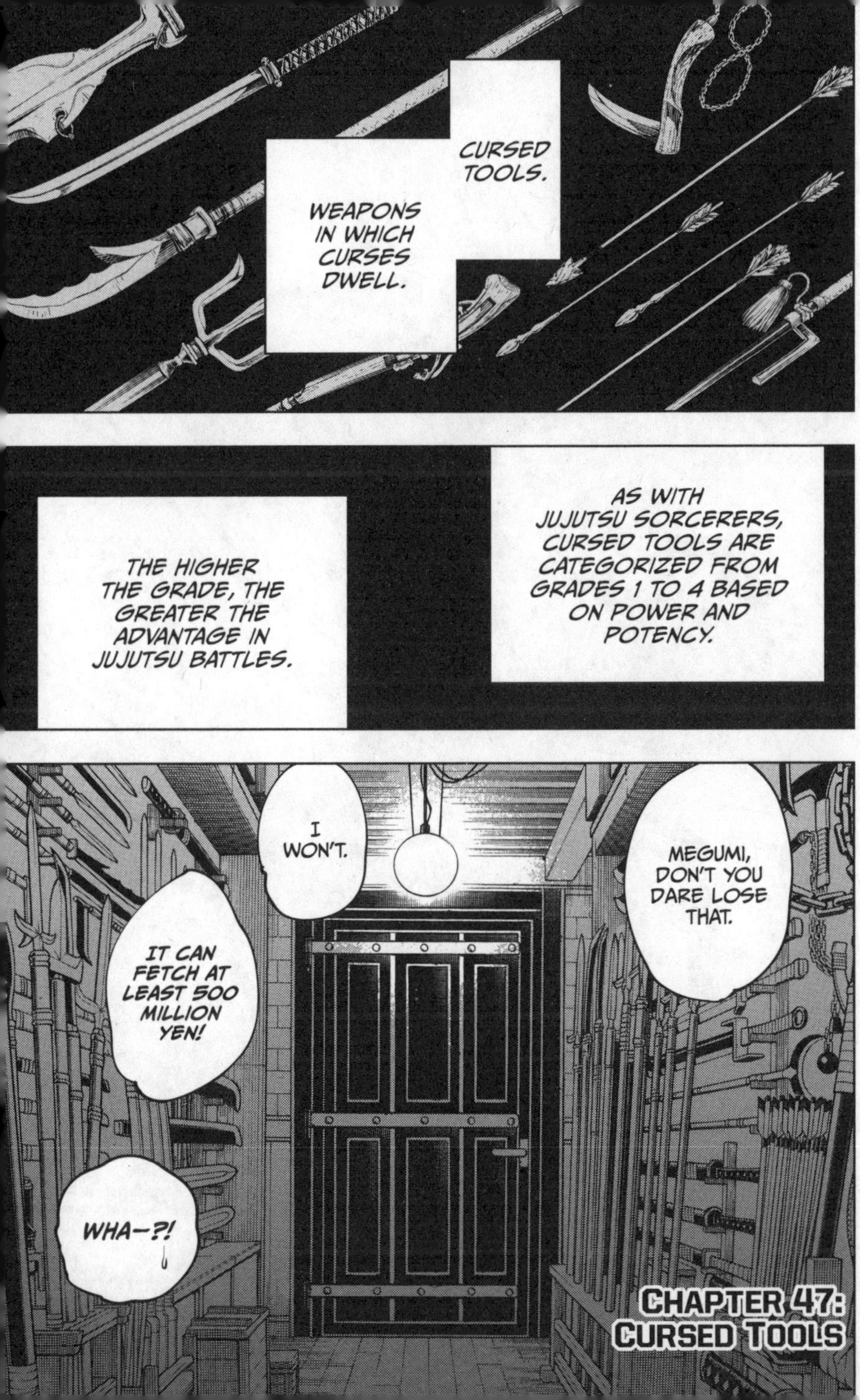
CURSED TOOLS.
WEAPONS IN WHICH CURSES DWELL.
AS WITH JUJUTSU SORCERERS, CURSED TOOLS ARE CATEGORIZED FROM GRADES 1 TO 4 BASED ON POWER AND POTENCY.
THE HIGHER THE GRADE, THE GREATER THE ADVANTAGE IN JUJUTSU BATTLES.
MEGUMI, DON'T YOU DARE LOSE THAT.
I WON'T.
IT CAN FETCH AT LEAST 500 MILLION YEN!
WHA-?!
CHAPTER 47: CURSED TOOLS

SPECIAL GRADE CURSED TOOL
FWIP
FWAK

PLAYFUL CLOUD
FWSSH
KA-KA-KA-KRA-KRASH

SPLAASH
INDEED, THAT IS NOT BAD.
DIVINE DOG

TOTALITY!
WITH THE EXCEPTION OF UNKNOWN ABYSS— FUSHIGURO'S EXTENSION CURSED TECHNIQUE...
...HIS TEN SHIKIGAMI CANNOT BE SUMMONED AGAIN WHEN COMPLETELY DESTROYED.
HOWEVER, THE CURSED TECHNIQUE AND POWER THE SHIKIGAMI LEAVES BEHIND WHEN DESTROYED...
...ARE INHERITED BY THE OTHER SHIKIGAMI.

SPLASH SPLASH SPLASH
SHNK

IT'S FAST... IS IT GOING AFTER MY INJURED ARM FIRST?
THE JUJUTSU SORCERER CHILD IS IN THE WOODS.
TP TP TP
KRI NG

THE BOY'S SWORD!!

MAKI!!
FWP
FWP

SHWIK

NEVER MAKE ME USE A THREE-SECTION STAFF AGAIN!
IT'S SO HARD TO USE!!
ONCE YOU GET USED TO IT, IT'S USE—
MEGUMI!!
HEH

THUNK
MAKI!!
DAMMIT! IT'S BECAUSE I MESSED UP!
I AIMED FOR THE HEART...
WHAT WONDERFUL REACTIONS.
JUJUTSU SORCERERS ARE INTERESTING. AND SO EMOTIONAL TOO.
EVERY TIME ONE OF THEIR ALLIES GETS HURT, THEY LEAVE NEW OPENINGS.

PSHH
GUH...
IS IT DESTROYED? NO, MEGUMI DISPELLED HIS CURSED TECHNIQUE.
I WOULDN'T USE JUJUTSU ANYMORE IF I WERE YOU.

THE BUD I PLANTED IN YOU LOVES CURSED ENERGY.
THE MORE JUJUTSU YOU USE, THE DEEPER INTO YOU IT WILL GROW.
HOW NICE OF YOU TO EXPLAIN!
YOU'RE PLANNING ON KILLING ME ANYWAY, RIGHT?
I HEAR IT'S MORE EFFECTIVE...
...ONCE EXPLAINED.

FWING
FWING
YOU HAVE SOME NICE MOVES.
FWISH
FWISH
WHAM

BUT NOT AS SHARP AS BEFORE.
KRRRL
RRRL
I NEED TO USE EVERYTHING I'VE GOT! EVEN IF I GET RIPPED APART!
I CHOOSE WHO I SAVE, UNLIKE THE OTHERS.
I'M BEARING THE LEAST BURDEN! THAT'S WHY...
IT'S INEXCUSABLE THAT I BE THE FIRST TO GO DOWN!
RAAAAAHHHH

MEGUMI.
THAT'S ENOUGH.
WE'VE DONE OUR JOB.
TIME TO TAG OUT!

YOU GOOD, ITADORI, MY FRIEND?!

WHAM
YEAH!

SUPPLEMENTARY INFO ③

Ten Shadows Technique

1. Divine Dogs (White & Black)
2. Toad
3. Great Serpent
4. Nue
5. Max Elephant
6. ??
7. ??
8. ??
9. ??
10. ??

Extra ② + ④ The Well's Unknown Abyss

THE WELL'S UNKNOWN ABYSS IS SOMETHING FUSHIGURO MADE UP USING TEN SHADOWS TECHNIQUE AS A BASE, SO IT CAN BE DESTROYED WITHOUT CONSEQUENCE. (BUT IT IS VERY WEAK.) HOWEVER, IF EITHER ② OR ④ WERE TO BE DESTROYED, IT WOULD NO LONGER BE POSSIBLE TO SUMMON IT. NUMBERS ② AND ④ DO NOT FUSE USING TOTALITY. THERE ARE SEPARATE RULES WHEN SHIKIGAMI INHERIT OTHER SHIKIGAMI.

Chapter 48: Black Flash

YOU GOOD, ITADORI, MY FRIEND?
YEAH!
STOP, ITADORI!
THAT'S NOT THE KIND OF ENEMY WE–
KOFF! KOFF!
PANDA.
SPLASH
YEAH.
VNN
!

TAKE THOSE TWO AND GET OUT OF THE CURTAIN.
ACCORDING TO NISHIMIYA, IT'S SPECIFICALLY DESIGNED TO COUNTER SATORU GOJO. YOU SHOULD BE ABLE TO GO IN AND OUT NO PROBLEM.
WAIT! EVEN YOU WON'T—
FUSHI-GURO.
DON'T WORRY.
PLEASE.

YOU SEE IT TOO.
HE'S BEGINNING TO SPREAD HIS WINGS. HE MUST FIND HIS OWN WAY.
THAT IS WHERE HE STANDS.
GUH
I'LL KILL YOU IF YOU DIE AGAIN!!
ALL RIGHT, LET'S GO!
PANDAAASH!!
I GUESS I CAN'T GO DYING ON YA THEN.

SPLISH
ITADORI, I WON'T INTERFERE.
NOT UNTIL...
...YOU SUCCESSFULLY USE...
...BLACK FLASH!
BAM?!
NO MATTER WHAT HAPPENS, IF YOU CAN'T USE BLACK FLASH...
...THEN I'LL WATCH YOU DIE!
GOT IT!

SUKUNA'S VESSEL... AND WHO'S THAT GUY? HE CERTAINLY HAS AN AURA ABOUT HIM.
BUT JUDGING ONLY BY HIS OVERALL CURSED ENERGY...
HE'S UNDOUBT-EDLY...
...WEAKER THAN ME.
BUT HE'S GOT A STRONG PRESENCE. MAYBE HIS CURSED TECHNIQUE IS POWERFUL. I CAN'T MAKE A CARELESS MOVE. PLUS, THIS MYSTERIOUS BLACK FLASH...
KRKK
SO, WHAT'S YOUR MOVE?

YOU...
...CAN TALK?
THERE'S SOMETHING I WANT TO ASK YOU.
IS THERE A CURSE IN YOUR GROUP...
...WITH A HUMAN FORM AND A PATCHWORK FACE?
VNN VNN
VNN
VNN
VNN
AND IF I SAID...
...THERE IS?

KRR

DUDUSHH
WHAK
WHAK
YOU'RE SMART TO CLOSE THE DISTANCE.
I COMMEND YOU FOR THAT.

WHAP
WHAP
WHAP
BAP
HE'S FAST!
MORE AGILE THAN THE GIRL!!
BUT HIS STRENGTH IS DISAPPOINTING.

HIS BODY IS WIDE OPEN! HE'S UNDER-ESTIMATING ME SINCE I PULLED MY PUNCHES. NOW'S MY CHANCE!
BLACK FLASH!!

VWAPA
AM
CRAP!
FSH
FWISH
DUN
DUN
VNP
VP
VP

ITADORI, MY FRIEND.
FWAP
ANGER IS A VALUABLE TRIGGER FOR A JUJUTSU SORCERER.
THERE'VE BEEN INSTANCES WHERE PEOPLE HAVE BEEN PUT ON THEIR HEELS AFTER PROVOKING AN INFERIOR OPPONENT.
THE OPPOSITE IS NOT GOOD EITHER.
MISHANDLING CURSED ENERGY WHEN ANGERED...
...WASTES YOUR SKILLS, AND THE FIGHT WILL END IN DEFEAT.

YOUR FRIEND FUSHIGURO IS HURT.
AND WORST OF ALL, OUR BONDING TIME AS BEST FRIENDS WAS INTERRUPTED...
...SO I UNDERSTAND BETTER THAN ANYONE WHY YOU WOULD LOSE YOUR COOL.
BUT THAT ANGER IS NOT FOR YOU.
SUPPRESS IT, FOR NOW.
FW
A FALLING...
...OUT?

ANY MORE DISTRACTIONS?
NOPE.
THANK YOU SO MUCH...
MY BEST FRIEND—TODO!

BLACK FLASH...
WHEN AN IMPACT OF CURSED ENERGY IS APPLIED WITHIN 0.000001 SECONDS OF A PHYSICAL HIT, A DISTORTION IN SPACE IS BORN.
THE IMPACT IS EQUAL TO A NORMAL HIT TO THE POWER OF 2.5.
THERE IS NOT A SINGLE JUJUTSU SORCERER WHO CAN USE IT AT WILL.
HOW-EVER...
FOR THOSE WHO HAVE EXPERIENCED BLACK FLASH, AS COMPARED TO THOSE WHO HAVE NOT...
...THEIR UNDER-STANDING OF THE ESSENCE OF CURSED ENERGY IS IMMEASURABLE.

FWOO
WHAT INCREDIBLE CONCENTRATION!
WHEN AN IMPACT OF CURSED ENERGY IS APPLIED WITHIN 0.000001 SECONDS OF A PHYSICAL HIT...
SPACE IS DISTORTED AND...

BLACK FLASH
CURSED ENERGY FLASHES BLACK!
WHA- ?!

THERE IT IS.

WHAT TO DO ABOUT BLACK FLASH??!

CHAPTER 49:
CONSTRAINED

JUJUTSU KAISEN

THERE IT IS.

VNN
VNN
VNN
VNN
VNN
THAT WAS... BLACK FLASH?!
WHAT? THIS IS MY CURSED ENERGY, RIGHT?
YOU GOT TO TASTE A *SAMPLE* OF YOUR CURSED ENERGY.
!!
SPLISH

UNTIL NOW, IT'S LIKE YOU'VE BEEN PUTTING INGREDIENTS...
...YOU'RE NOT FAMILIAR WITH INTO A POT AND COOKING HAPHAZARDLY.
BUT WITH ***BLACK FLASH***, YOU'VE GAINED THE ***INGREDIENT*** THAT IS CURSED ENERGY. AS A CHEF...
...OR IN THIS CASE, A JUJUTSU SORCERER, YOU'RE ON A DIFFERENT LEVEL THAN YOU WERE JUST THREE SECONDS AGO.
CONGRATU-LATIONS...
...BROTHER.
YOU...
...WILL BE STRONG!

I WAS TOLD THAT SUKUNA'S VESSEL WAS AN INEXPERIENCED JUJUTSU SORCERER.
PLUS THERE'S THIS MYSTERIOUS MAN.
KRK KRK
KRK KRK
THERE'S SOMETHING DIFFERENT ABOUT THESE TWO COMPARED TO THE REST.
KRZ
IT CAN HEAL ITSELF?!
CURSED SPIRITS ARE MADE FROM CURSED ENERGY.
THEY'RE DIFFERENT FROM US. THEY CAN EASILY HEAL THEMSELVES WITHOUT USING HIGH-LEVEL REVERSE CURSED TECHNIQUE.
IT'S CHILD'S PLAY FOR A SPECIAL GRADE.

BUT ITS CURSED ENERGY IS UNDOUBTEDLY WEAKENED.
IF WE CAN GET ITS HEAD, THEN IT'S GAME OVER.
FSH FSH
SO... SHALL WE GET COOKING ?!
BAM

GRCH GRCH
FOR YOU TWO...
...IT SEEMS THAT...
...I NEED TO TRY...
...A LITTLE HARDER!

WHAT AN ATTACK RANGE!
DON'T BE SCARED! IT SACRIFICES POWER AND SPEED IN EXCHANGE!

POW
POW
POW
WHAM

WHAT A HEAVY HIT! IT'S NOT QUITE AS HEAVY AS THE BLACK FLASH HIT FROM EARLIER.
HOWEVER, INDIVIDUALLY THEY HAVE ENOUGH POWER TO HURT ME.
TODO! LET'S SYNC UP OUR TIMING BETTER!
GOTCHA!
FWOOP

OUR FOOTING!
!!!
WE UNDER-ESTIMATED IT! WITH THIS AMOUNT OF MASS...
...I THOUGHT IT WAS MA-NIPULATING PHYSICAL BRANCHES WITH ITS CURSED ENERGY.
BUT IT'S THE EMBODIMENT OF CURSED ENERGY! IT MADE THE ILLUSION REAL WITH JUST ITS CURSED ENERGY!
THAT'S A SPECIAL GRADE FOR YOU!
FSSHHHHH
I'LL TEACH YOU...
...TO APPRE-CIATE THE LAND.

TWK
TWK
ATTACKING WHILE WE'RE FALLING! THAT'S NOT FAIR! HOWEVER...
BROTHER!!
VWW
WHAM

WOOOOSH
THEY DODGED IT?! BUT WHAT IS THIS FEELING?
!!

FSSHH
YOU SHOULD BE MORE TRUE TO YOURSELF, HANAMI.
FSHHH
I'M NOT TRYING TO BE ANYTHING ELSE.
I'M NOT SAYING YOU'RE LYING.
I KNOW WHY YOU FIGHT.
BUT AS LONG AS WE'RE FIGHTING...
FSHHH
...WHY NOT TRY TO ENJOY IT?
FSHH

IS IT FUN FOR YOU, MAHITO?
YEAH, BUT...
THE PLEASURE I FEEL WHILE FIGHTING...
...DIDN'T MOTIVATE ME MUCH UNTIL RECENTLY.
BEFORE I REALIZED IT, ALL THE DECEIT, CHEATING AND KILLING...
...LEFT ME SATIATED.

JUST LIKE HUMANS EAT, SLEEP AND RAPE...
...CURSES MANIFEST INSTINCTIVE BEHAVIORS AS WELL.
WE MIGHT HAVE GAINED REASONING...
...BUT THAT DOESN'T MEAN WE SHOULD DENY OUR IMPULSES.
SPIRIT IS A BLEND OF IMPULSE AND REASON.
YOU SHOULDN'T BE TOLD BY OTHERS HOW TO BALANCE THE TWO.
YOUR SPIRIT FEELS A LITTLE CONSTRAINED.
HANAMI, I HAVE A FEELING...
FSH FSH FSH FSH
YOU'RE MUCH STRONGER!

WOOOM
FOOSH
HHH
KS

MAHITO!
RIGHT NOW...!

...I'M HAVING FUN...
...FIGHTING!
YOU ALL RIGHT, BROTHER?
NO PROBLEM!
THERE YOU GO!
WELL THEN...
...I'M GONNA RELEASE...
...MY CURSED TECHNIQUE!!
UM... DIDN'T YOU USE IT EARLIER?
(ITADORI)

POP QUIZ JUJUTSU ASSESSMENT

Picture 1

Question 2
(answer required)

Use picture 1 and finish the drawing with the correct patterns on Hanami.
(15 points)

IN THIRD GRADE, I BEAT UP A HIGH SCHOOLER WITH A BAD ATTITUDE.
EVEN IF HE'S OLDER, A BAD ATTITUDE IS A BAD ATTITUDE.
THE OPPONENT IS MOCKING ME, AND I FEEL LIKE I'M BEING MOCKED.
AT THAT MOMENT, THE BELL FOR THE FIGHT HAS RUNG.
CHAPTER 50: FEELING
IT'S NOT FUN.
BEATING UP A BORING GUY IS, AS EXPECTED, BORING.
WIGGLE
HEY, KID!!
WAY TO GO!!

WHAT KIND OF GIRLS ARE YOU INTO?
KRKK
I HAD A FEELING...
...THAT I WOULDN'T BE BORED FOR LONG.
WHO ARE YOU?

I'M GONNA RELEASE MY CURSED TECHNIQUE!!
UM... DIDN'T YOU USE IT EARLIER?
THERE'S NO TIME TO GO INTO THE DETAILS!
BAM
THERE'S ONLY ONE THING TO SAY...
DON'T STOP!!
BAM BAM BAM BAM
BELIEVE IN ME!!
GOTCHA! THAT'S TWO!
(ITADORI)

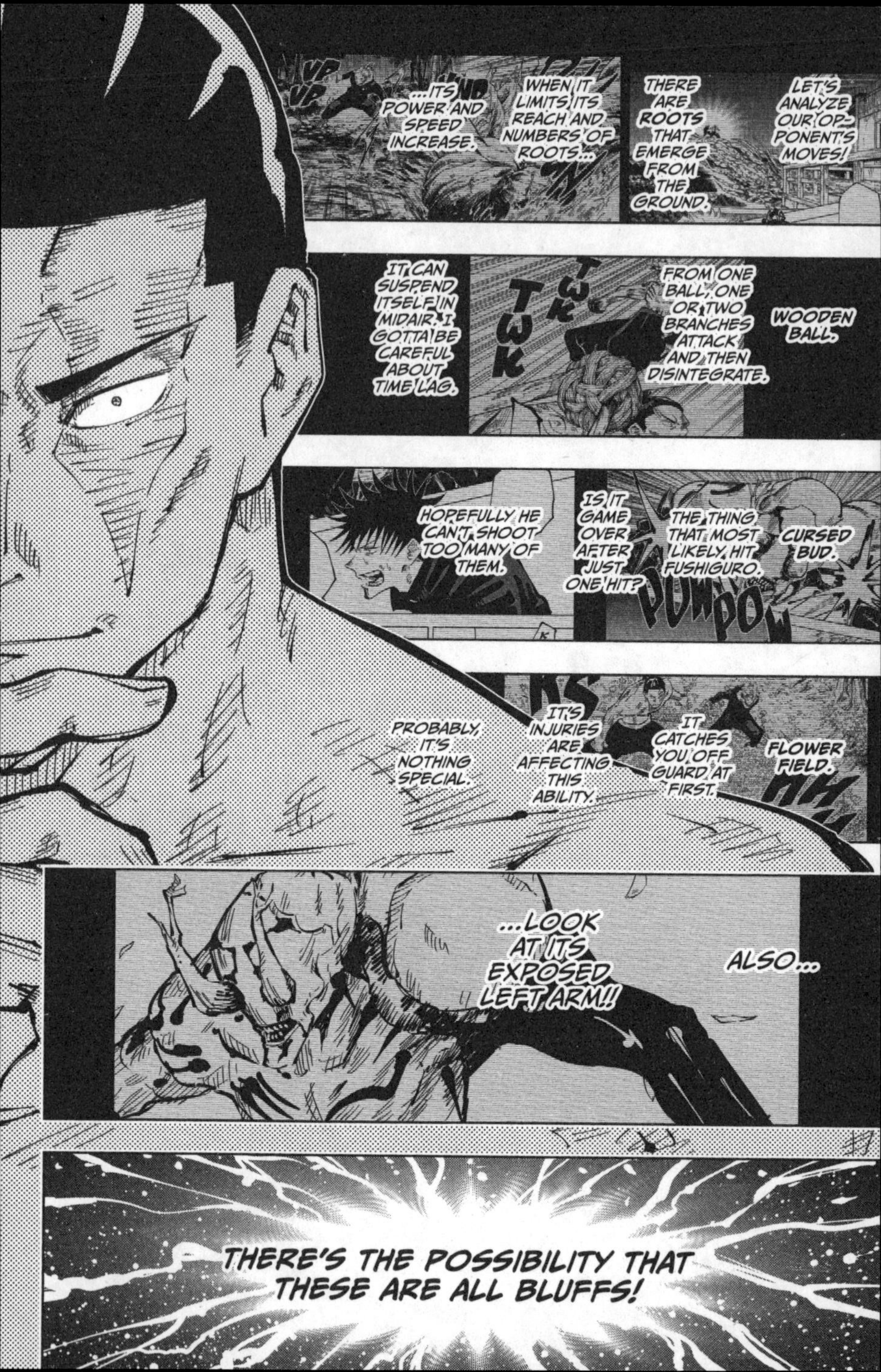

LET'S ANALYZE OUR OPPONENT'S MOVES!
THERE ARE ROOTS THAT EMERGE FROM THE GROUND.
WHEN IT LIMITS ITS REACH AND NUMBERS OF ROOTS...
...ITS POWER AND SPEED INCREASE.
WOODEN BALL.
FROM ONE BALL, ONE OR TWO BRANCHES ATTACK AND THEN DISINTEGRATE.
IT CAN SUSPEND ITSELF IN MIDAIR. I GOTTA BE CAREFUL ABOUT TIME LAG.
CURSED BUD.
THE THING THAT MOST LIKELY HIT FUSHIGURO.
IS IT GAME OVER AFTER JUST ONE HIT?
HOPEFULLY HE CAN'T SHOOT TOO MANY OF THEM.
FLOWER FIELD.
IT CATCHES YOU OFF GUARD AT FIRST.
IT'S INJURIES ARE AFFECTING THIS ABILITY.
PROBABLY, IT'S NOTHING SPECIAL.
ALSO...
...LOOK AT ITS EXPOSED LEFT ARM!!
THERE'S THE POSSIBILITY THAT THESE ARE ALL BLUFFS!

IT'S JUST A MATTER OF NOT LETTING IT USE ITS CURSED TECHNIQUE!
EVEN CONSIDERING ANY SURPRISES, WITH MY BRAIN CPU POSSESSING AN IQ OF 53,000*—THE EXPECTED OUTCOME SHOULD BE...
VICTORY!
*SELF-PROCLAIMED
BECAUSE...
...I'M NOT ALONE.
BROTHER!
IT'S BECAUSE I HAVE YOU!

OOPS!
VWISH
VWISH
VWOOOM

FWOSH
TODO!!
WHAK
GRK
WHAP
ONE DOWN.
CLAP

THWK
THWK
TINK
!!!
TODO!!

I SEE.
IT'S A SIMPLE...
...BUT TROUBLE-SOME CURSED TECHNIQUE.
KRPP
YUP, MY CURSED TECHNIQUE LETS ME TRADE PLACES WITH SOMEONE ELSE...
BOOGIE WOOGIE!

TODO!
BY THE WAY...
SHH...
LET'S FINISH THIS BEFORE IT GETS USED TO IT.
CLAP-PING...
CLAP
...MY HANDS...
CLAP
...IS THE TRIGGER!
CLAP

CLAP
CLAP
CLAP
NK
TH-
THU
THE DIFFERENCE IN BODY SIZE... THE DIFFERENCE AFTER THEY SWITCH IS HUGE!!
SWITCHING WITH ME AND SWITCHING WITH SUKUNA'S VESSEL—IT'S AFFECTING MY JUDGMENT!!
THIS ISN'T GOOD! I...

CLAP
CLAP
...CAN'T...
CLAP
CLAP
CLAP
CLAP

CLAP
...ESCAPE!!
CLAP
CLAP

ST
MBL
!!
HERE IT COMES AGAIN!
THE RECORD HOLDER FOR CONSECUTIVE USES OF BLACK FLASH ...
...AS TOLD BY KENTO NANAMI...
KLAK

USING BLACK FLASH CONSECUTIVELY ISN'T AMAZING.
USING IT MORE THAN TWICE, IT WOULD BE DIFFICULT TO DO CONSECUTIVELY OR ON THE SAME DAY.
AND IT DOESN'T MATTER IF THE FIRST TIME WAS DONE OUT OF PURE LUCK OR SKILL.
WHEN SUCCESSFULLY USING BLACK FLASH, JUJUTSU SORCERERS ARE IN A ZONE SIMILAR TO WHAT ATHLETES EXPERIENCE.
THE TYPICAL THOUGHT PROCESS OF MANIPULATING CURSED ENERGY BECOMES LIKE BREATHING.
HOW SHOULD I PUT IT...? IT'S LIKE THE FEELING THAT YOU'RE THE CENTER THAT EVERYTHING ELSE REVOLVES AROUND.

MY RECORD?
FWOO
FOUR.
I WAS LUCKY.
BLACK FLASH
BROTHER! I ALWAYS GET THIS FEELING ABOUT YOU!
KRSH
KRSH
KRSH
KRSH

BLACK FLASH
BLACK FLASH
THREE TIMES!
DON'T GET COCKY.
FSH

THEY'RE GOING TO SWITCH PLACES!
I NEED TO BE CAREFUL OF...
CL
AP
FSH
...SUKUNA'S...

THEY DIDN'T SWITCH!
A CLAP...
...DOESN'T NECESSARILY MEAN I'M USING MY CURSED TECHNIQUE.
THIS IS THE SAME FEELING I HAD WHEN I THOUGHT MY BORE-DOM WOULD END!!
IT'S SIMPLE BUT EFFECTIVE, RIGHT?
BLACK FLASH

INTERVIEWER INO

CHAPTER 51: A FLOWER OFFERING

KZZT KZZT
KZZT KZZT
FWSH

FSH
FSH
VOON
FWT

CL AP
ZWOOM
WHAM
WHA

KRAAACK
IT'S ANTICIPATING AND ATTACKING WHEN WE SWITCH! IT'S GETTING USED TO TODO'S CURSED TECHNIQUE!
HOWEVER, THE BLACK FLASH BARRAGE EARLIER DEFINITELY DID SOME DAMAGE.
WE CAN EXORCISE IT! TOGETHER!
THIS IS THE FIRST TIME I'VE BEEN HURT SO MUCH...!!
EVEN SO!!

HEH HEH HEH
HEH
HEH
HEH
THE THRILL OF THE FIGHT...
HEH
HEH
HEH
HEH
HEH
...REMAINS STRONG!
HEH
TINK
TINK
CL
AP

POP
WHAT HE SAID AT THE START OF OUR FIGHT ABOUT HIS CURSED TECHNIQUE WASN'T THE WHOLE TRUTH! HE CAN MAKE OTHERS SWAP PLACES AS WELL!
TODO!
HE WAS PROTECTING ME!

NOT TO WORRY, BROTHER! BY USING EVERYTHING I'VE GOT TO HARDEN MY BODY AND CURSED ENERGY...
...I'LL BE ABLE TO REPEL THOSE BUDS EASILY!
YOU SURE?
TA-
TAKADA!
VOOOM

YOU REMEMBER FUSHIGURO'S WOUNDS?
OF COURSE I DO!
THOSE ARE THE SAME CURSED BUDS THAT ARE COMING FOR ME AS WE SPEAK!
THAT'S WHY I—
BUT FUSHIGURO'S BUDS...
...GREW A BIT.
HEH
DID IT GROW BY SUCKING BLOOD?
IT'S POSSIBLE. BUT THE OPPONENT IS A CURSED SPIRIT. WHAT'S MORE LIKELY?
TICK TOCK
TICK TOCK
TICK TOCK
DING!
CURSED ENERGY!
TIME ELAPSED— 0.01 SECONDS.

FWOO
BAP BA BA BAP
!!
KRCH
KRCH
HE DISENGAGED HIS CURSED ENERGY AT THE LAST MOMENT! HE MUST HAVE REALIZED THAT CURSED BUDS GET STRONGER WHEN THE PROTECTIVE CURSED ENERGY IS GREATER!
I'LL HAVE TO THANK HER AT THE NEXT...
...NATIONAL FAN APPRECIATION MEET AND GREET.
KRCH
FWP
FWAK

HEY, SPECIAL GRADE!
VWA
ACK
YOU MUST HAVE REALIZED THAT I DIDN'T TELL YOU THE WHOLE TRUTH.
SO THERE'S ONE MORE THING YOU NEED TO THINK ABOUT.
THE APPLICABLE TARGETS OF MY BOOGIE WOOGIE CURSED TECHNIQUE!
ARE THE TARGETS I CAN SWITCH LIMITED TO...
...LIVING THINGS? NOPE!
MY CURSED TECHNIQUE IS ALSO EFFECTIVE ON OBJECTS, SUCH AS CURSED PUPPETS. SO, THE ANSWER IS...

ANYTHING THAT POSSESSES CURSED ENERGY ABOVE A CERTAIN LEVEL.
HEY, SPECIAL GRADE, HAVE YOU NOTICED YET?
WE'RE BACK...
...HERE.
SOME-THING'S...
...LYING IN SLEEP.

CLAP

MAKI'S SPECIAL GRADE CURSED TOOL IS IN THE RIVERBED.
THE BRANCHES ON ITS FACE...
...ARE INCREDIBLY VULNERABLE TO ATTACK!
POP
SPLASH
THE RIVER?!
WHAT THE HECK DID I SWITCH PLACES WITH?!
SPECIAL GRADE...
...CURSED TOOL!

PLAYFUL CLOUD!

VWSHH
TP
TP
TP
SHRIVEL
THAT WAS A HIT FROM A SPECIAL GRADE CURSED TOOL INFUSED WITH MY CURSED ENERGY, BUT IT'S STILL NOT ENOUGH!!

KRAK
KRAK
KRAK KRRK KRRRK
PLANTS DO NOT EMBRACE CURSED ENERGY.
MY LEFT ARM TAKES THE LIFE ENERGY OF PLANTS...
...AND CHANGES IT INTO CURSED ENERGY. IT DOESN'T COME TO ME.
IT ALL GOES TO THIS FLOWER OFFERING.

GLARE
I WOULD HAVE LIKED TO AVOID USING THIS.

TODO!
TP
STAY AWAY, BROTHER! IT'S GONNA BE AN INCREDIBLE BLAST OF CURSED ENERGY!
HOWEVER, WITH YOUR CURSED TECHNIQUE, AVOIDING MY ATTACK WOULD BE EASY.
SO, I'M LEFT WITH...
DOMAIN ...
...EX-
WOOOSH

!!
THE CUR-TAIN!

SUPPLEMENTARY INFO ④

Hanami is super tough.
Jogo is technically stronger (considering how their elemental types match up) than Hanami.
However, if he were ever to receive five of Itadori's Black Flash attacks on top of Todo's cursed energy-infused Playful Cloud strike (as Hanami has at this point), he would die instantly.

KREEE
CHAPTER 52:
NONSTANDARD
KZZT
KZZT
KZZT
KREEE

KRAK
FSH
I SEE.
THAT'S A PRETTY NICE SOUND CONSIDERING THERE'S NO AMP.

THE GEEZER HIMSELF IS THE AMP!
HIS CURSED TECHNIQUE AMPLIFIES THE MELODIES HE PLAYS AND LAUNCHES THEM AS CURSED ENERGY!
HE'S A PREDICTABLE MIDRANGE FIGHTER.
HE OBVIOUSLY DOESN'T WANT PEOPLE CLOSING IN ON HIM.
I'LL MAKE A WALLET OUT OF YOU!
A WALLET INFUSED WITH THE ESSENCE OF OLD MAN STINK!

FSH
UNDERSTOOD. NISHIMIYA, YOU STAY THERE WITH SHOKO.
DON'T WORRY, MIWA IS WITH MEI.
THANK GOODNESS WE STILL HAVE RECEPTION.
I GUESS THAT MAKES SENSE CONSIDERING THIS CURTAIN'S EFFECT.
A CURSE USER IS HERE AT THE SCHOOL. OR SOMEONE WHO'S WORKING WITH CURSED SPIRITS.
HE'S PROBABLY RIGHT.

HUH?
KSSSHT

I THOUGHT I HAD YOU FOR SURE.
A HUMAN!
SIGH
THERE I GO AGAIN...
DOOM...
IT'S NICE, RIGHT?
JUZO MADE IT FOR ME. YOU PROBABLY MET HIM EARLIER.

HE SAID I'M UNRE-LIABLE...
...SO EVEN MY KATANA SHOULD HOLD MY HAND.
SO...
WHAT ARE YOU GONNA GIVE ME?
I BET...
...YOU'RE NOT TOO POPULAR WITH THE LADIES.
TALKING ONLY ABOUT YOURSELF.

HAND OVER ALL YOUR MONEY!
WHAT MAKES YOU THINK YOU'VE GOT WHAT IT TAKES FOR A SHAKEDOWN?
SHUT UP! WHY'RE YOU PICKING A FIGHT AT A TIME LIKE THIS?!
YOU TWO!
WHOA!
SO MANY GIRLS!
I'M SO POPULAR!
ARE YOU EVEN LISTENING?
I'LL BACK YOU UP!
JUST MAKE SURE YOU DON'T GET CAUGHT IN SOME FRIENDLY FIRE.
WHY YOU—!

THE CURTAIN IS GONE!
FOR REAL?!
HAS IT EVEN BEEN 30 MINUTES?
I'M OUTTA HERE!
FWOOSH
WHAT WAS UP WITH THAT GUY?
HEY, HEY, HEY, HEY!
I SPY A GOOD LOOKIN' HANGER RACK.

WELL THEN...

FWOOOO
WHERE TO GO FIRST?
IT SEEMS THAT....
...OUR TIME IS UP.
GOJO SENSEI?!

YUJI'S GOTTEN WAY STRONGER!
I SEE, AOI! THAT MAKES SENSE. HE WORKS WELL WITH YUJI.
THEY SHOULD BE OKAY EVEN IF THEY'RE UP AGAINST A SPECIAL GRADE.
IN THAT CASE, LET'S START...
FWP
...WITH YOU.

RACK! RACK!
TP
DON'T KILL HIM!!
GRSH
GSH
GSH
GSH

THUD
YEAH, WE NEED THIS ONE ALIVE FOR QUESTION-ING.
CAN'T LET HIM DIE.
HEAL HIM FOR ME, WOULDJA?
KRK
THE GUY THAT WAS WITH UTAHIME IS GONE. SEEMS THAT RUNNING AWAY WAS AN OPTION FROM THE START.
ALL THAT'S LEFT IS THE SPECIAL GRADE, WHO'S ALSO GOOD AT RUNNING AWAY.
YUJI AND THE OTHERS ARE A LITTLE FAR AWAY. IN THAT CASE...
LET'S GET...
CURSED TECHNIQUE LAPSE: BLUE
CURSED TECHNIQUE REVERSAL: RED
...A LITTLE CRAZY.

VOON
TIME TO LEAVE.
I'M NOT SO PROUD THAT I WOULD GO UP AGAINST SATORU GOJO.
DON'T YOU DARE!
VOON VOON
WHAT IS IT YOU GUYS WANT?!
BROTHER!
VSH
TODO!
WHY'RE YOU STOPPING ME?!
DON'T GO ANY FURTHER.
OR YOU'LL BE COL-LATERAL DAMAGE!

HOLLOW PURPLE

FWOON
VWOOOM

RMMBL
RM
MBL
AS EXPECTED ...
GASP
HEH HEH HEH
HE'S NON-STANDARD.
I CAN'T EVEN TELL IF IT'S EXORCISED.

YAA
AY!
WE ALL GOOD!
SHUT UP!
OW! IT HURTS SO BAD!!
AS IF...
I WONDER IF HANAMI IS OKAY.
MISSION ACCOMPLISHED.
TO BE CONTINUED

JUJUTSU KAISEN

reads from right to left, starting in the upper-right corner. Japanese is read from right to left, meaning that action, sound effects and word-balloon order are completely reversed from English order.

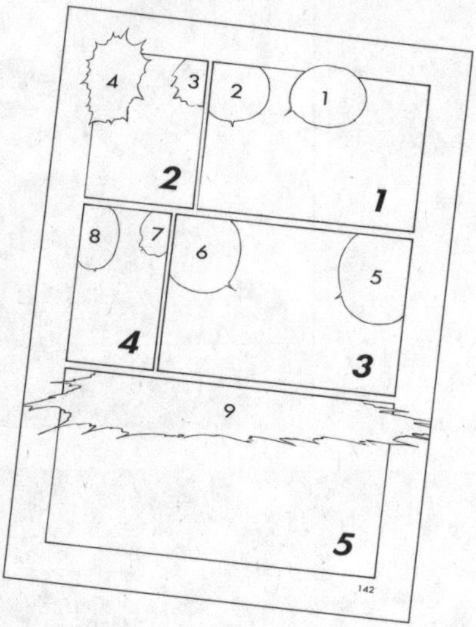